Try It with Triangles

Learning to Put Triangles Together to Form Other Shapes

Zelda King

Math for the REAL World™

Rosen Classroom™

New York

Published in 2004, 2010 by The Rosen Publishing Group, Inc.
29 East 21st Street, New York, NY 10010

Revised Edition

Book Design: Michael Tsanis

Photo Credits: Cover, p. 5 (yield sign) © Carolyn Ross/Index Stock; cover (glass patterns) © Hot Ideas/ Index Stock; pp. 5 (square, rectangle, pendant flag), 6 (octagon, diamond) by Michael Tsanis; p. 7 © Frank Whitney/The Image Bank; pp. 8–9, 10–11, 12–13 by Michael Tsanis; p. 11 (inset) © Raymond Gehman/Corbis; p. 14 © Steve Mason/PhotoDisc.

ISBN: 978-0-8239-8873-0
6-pack ISBN: 978-0-8239-7382-8

Manufactured in the United States of America

CPSIA Compliance Information: Batch #CR514240RC: For further information contact Rosen Publishing, New York, New York at 1-800-237-9932.

Contents

What Is a Triangle?

A triangle is one of the four basic flat shapes. The other three are the rectangle, the square, and the circle.

All triangles have three sides and three corners, or **angles**. In fact, the word "triangle" means "three angles." However, all triangles are not exactly alike. Their angles may be large or small. Their sides may be different lengths.

Two triangles can be put together to make a rectangle or square. Look around, and you'll discover that these three shapes are all around us.

square
(two triangles)

triangle

triangle

rectangle
(two triangles)

Making Other Shapes with Triangles

Two triangles can make a square, a rectangle, or a **diamond**. Several triangles can be put together to make other shapes. Eight equal triangles can be put together to make a shape like a stop sign. This shape is called an **octagon**. The word "octagon" means "eight angles."

octagon
(eight triangles)

diamond
(two triangles)

A baseball field is called a "diamond" because it is shaped like a diamond.

Let's Draw with Triangles!

You can draw pictures using only triangles. It's easy to do. To draw a house, first put two triangles together to make a rectangle. Put a triangle on top, and the triangles become a house! Next to the house, you can draw a smaller house for the family dog. You can also draw a car with triangles.

You can even use triangles to draw trees and clouds!

Draw a Garden with Triangles

You might be surprised to discover that a garden has many things you can draw with triangles. If you look closely at the things that live and grow in a garden, you may see triangles in places you did not expect to find them. You can draw a flower or a leaf using triangles. You can draw a butterfly, too.

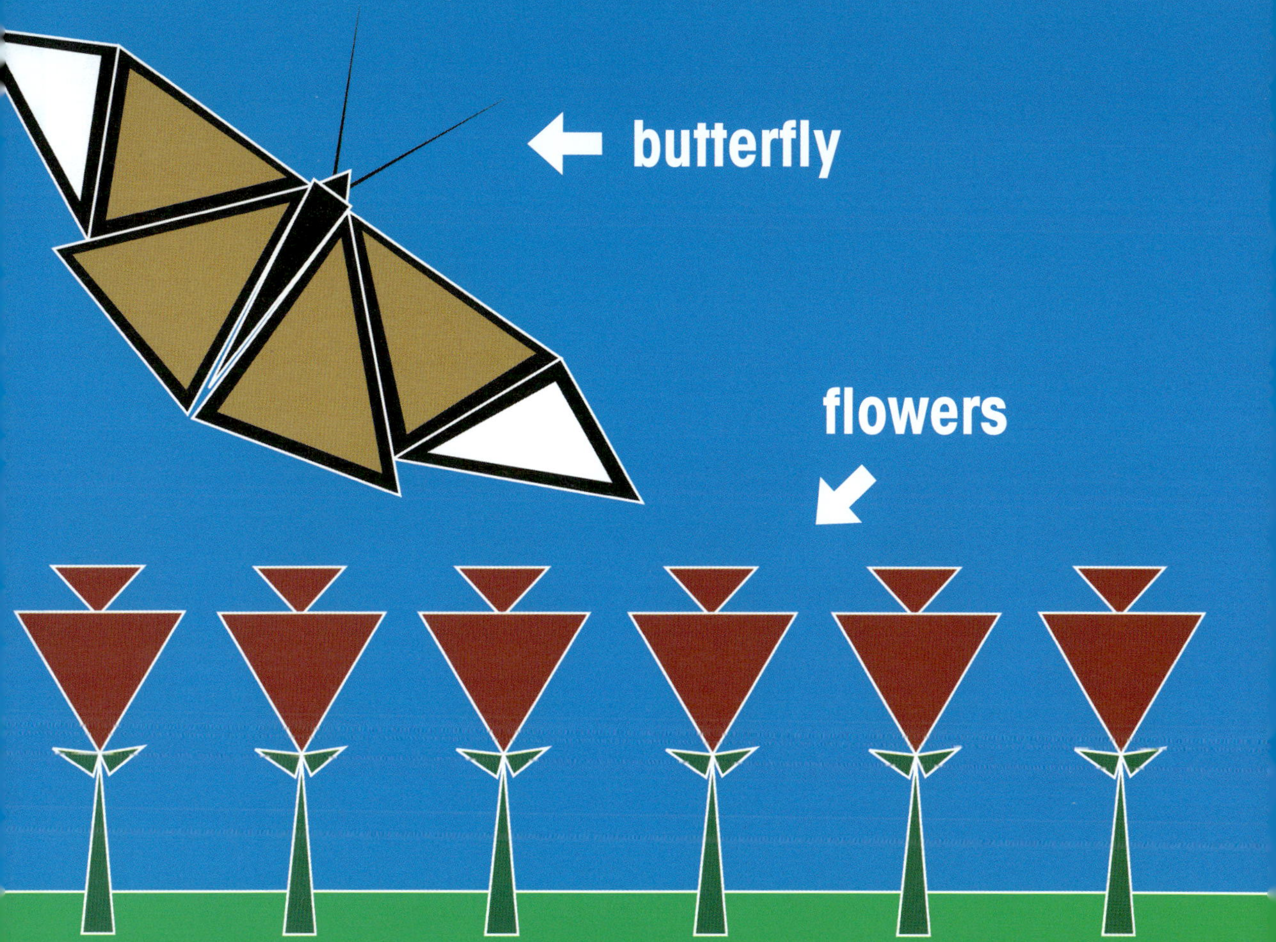

Visit a garden and see what else you can find to draw with triangles.

Draw Animals with Triangles

You can use triangles to draw animals from all around the world. You can draw a camel or an elephant from Africa. You can draw a buffalo from North America. You can draw a kangaroo from Australia, or a penguin from the South Pole!

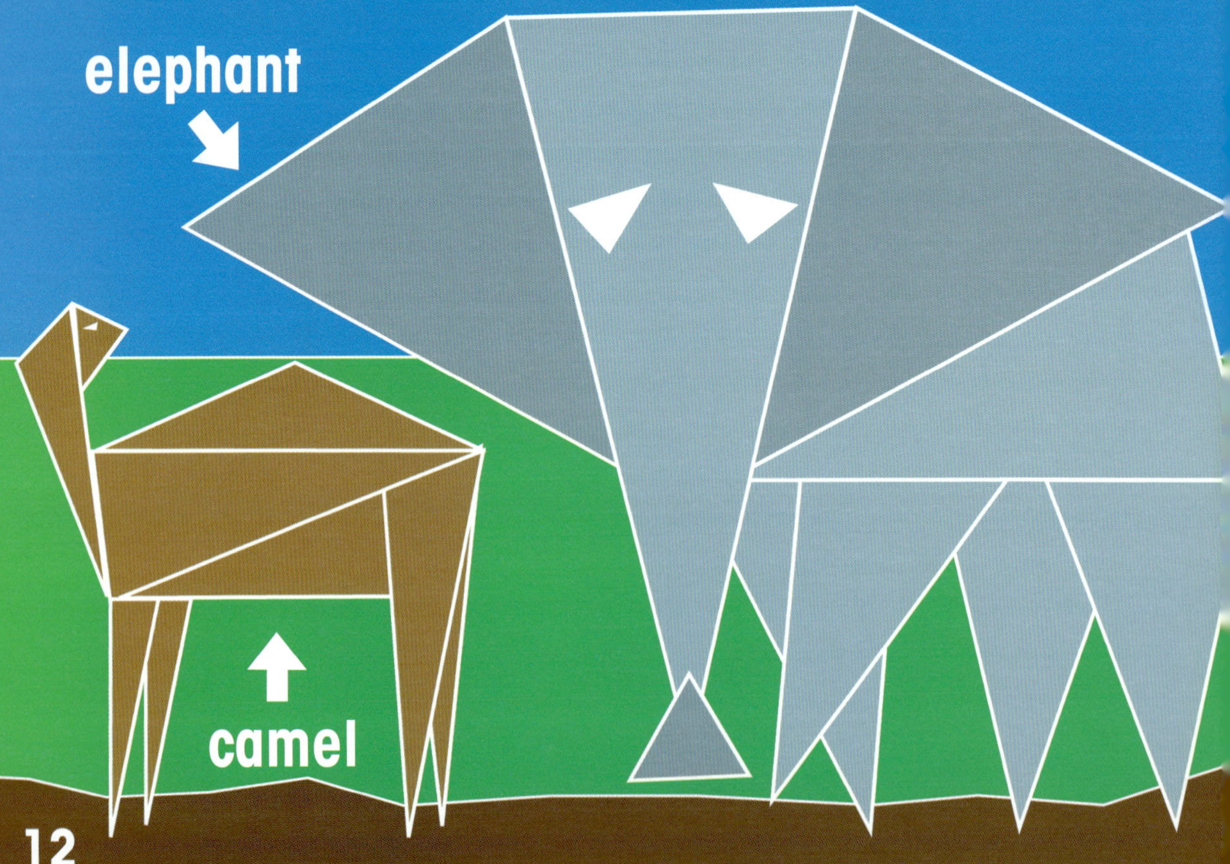

What is your favorite animal? See if you can draw it using only triangles.

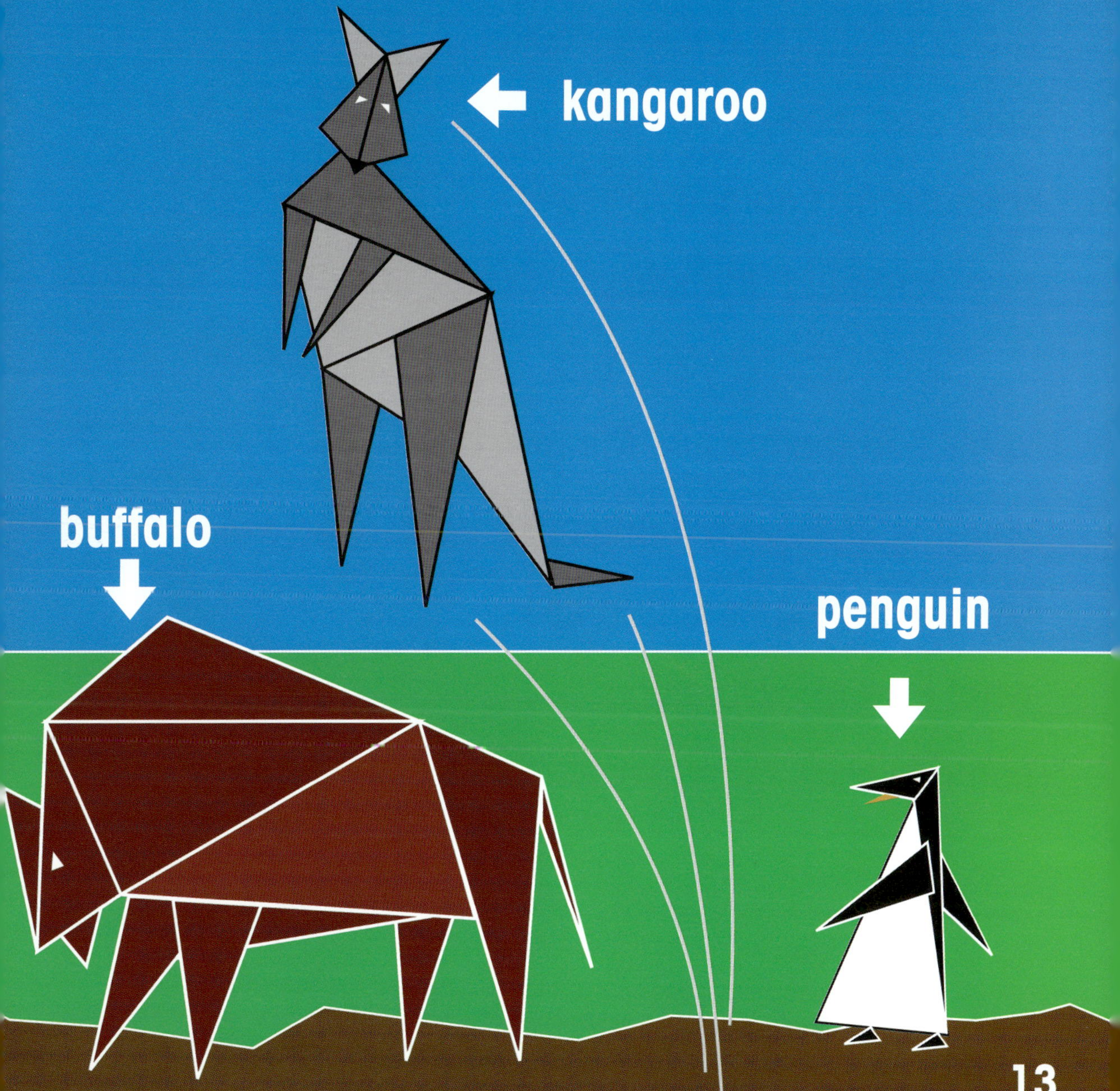

Be a Triangle Artist

You can **copy** some of the drawings in this book to make your own picture. You can draw a house and garden, a forest, or a parade of animals.

Look around you, and you'll find many other things you can draw with triangles. Use your **imagination** to see what kind of picture you can make!

Glossary

angle (AIN-guhl) A corner formed where two straight lines meet.

copy (KAH-pea) To make something that looks just like something else.

diamond (DIE-muhnd) The shape made when a square is turned so that one of its corners is at the bottom.

imagination (ih-ma-juh-NAY-shun) The power to dream up new things.

octagon (AHK-tuh-gahn) A shape that has eight angles and eight sides.

Index